PRO WRESTLING LEGENDS

CHELSEA HOUSE PUBLISHERS

Billy Kidman

Jacqueline Mudge

Chelsea House Publishers
Philadelphia

Produced by Chestnut Productions and Choptank Syndicate, Inc.

Editor and Picture Researcher: Mary Hull
Design and Production: Lisa Hochstein

CHELSEA HOUSE PUBLISHERS

Editor in Chief: Sally Cheney
Associate Editor in Chief: Kim Shinners
Production Manager: Pamela Loos
Art Director: Sara Davis
Director of Photography: Judy L. Hasday

Cover Photos: Howard Kernats Photography
            and The Acci'Dent

The Chelsea House World Wide Web site
address is http://www.chelseahouse.com

First Printing

1 3 5 7 9 8 6 4 2

Library of Congress Cataloging-in-Publication Data

Mudge, Jacqueline.
    Billy Kidman / Jacqueline Mudge.
        p. cm. — (Pro wrestling legends)
    Includes bibliographical references (p.) and index.
    ISBN 0–7910–6457–3 (alk. paper) — ISBN 0–7910–6458–1 (pbk. : alk. paper)
        1. Kidman, Billy, 1974– —Juvenile literature. 2. Wrestlers—United States—
    Biography—Juvenile literature. [1. Kidman, Bily, 1974– . 2. Wrestlers.] I. Title. II.
    Series.

    GV1196.K53 M83 2001
    796.812'092—dc21
    [B]
                                                            00–069410

Contents

1 OUT WITH THE OLD

This was the Monday night that the wrestling world had been waiting for, the night big changes would be taking place. For two weeks, World Championship Wrestling (WCW) executives Eric Bischoff and Vince Russo had been promising to usher in a new era for the federation. On April 10, 2000, the time had come for them to back their promise with action.

Actually, Bischoff and Russo had made *two* promises. The second was to Billy Kidman, and it had been made nearly four months earlier. Kidman was concerned that he wasn't getting the attention and top-level matches he wanted in WCW, and he was threatening to take his outstanding aerial and mat skills to another organization, perhaps the World Wrestling Federation (WWF). Bischoff and Russo, not wanting to lose Kidman, promised him a run at superstardom. Now, finally, Kidman was about to find out whether Russo and Bischoff would be true to their words.

"We're going to shake things up like they've never been shaken up before," Russo declared. That's exactly what he and Bischoff did.

When that night's broadcast of *Nitro* opened, most of WCW's top wrestlers were in the ring, waiting for Russo to show up

A new era was born in WCW on April 10, 2000, when Billy Kidman defeated Hulk Hogan in an impromptu match at Nitro.

for a nationally televised company meeting. When Russo arrived, he criticized the previous management within WCW and declared that effective immediately, there would be a new way of doing business in WCW. Then Bischoff came to the ring, hugged Russo, and declared that it was time for the Millionaire's Club of WCW—well-known competitors such as Hulk Hogan, Ric Flair, Sting, Lex Luger, and "Diamond" Dallas Page—to take a back seat to the New Blood.

"The good ol' boy network is out," Bischoff declared.

Kidman wasn't sure (yet) what all of this had to do with him. Certainly, he wasn't part of the "good ol' boy network." He was only 26 years old. He hadn't been part of the old regime's way of doing things, or any regime's way, for that matter. After all, he didn't even wrestle at Starrcade '99, the federation's most important card of the year. Still, Kidman couldn't help but wonder: *What are these guys up to? Weren't Russo and Bischoff themselves part of the old regime?* Indeed, they were.

But Russo and Bischoff weren't done for the night. As Page, Sting, and Luger watched the proceedings from the backstage area, Russo criticized former WCW World champion Ric Flair, one of the greatest wrestlers ever, then declared that all WCW titles had been vacated. Every champion had to give up his title. The message being delivered by Russo and Bischoff was clear: The selfish old veterans had been holding back the young stars, and it was going to stop.

Moments later, Hulk Hogan arrived at the arena, unaware of what he had missed. Sting filled him in. The "Hulkster" was enraged, and started looking for Bischoff.

Then Kidman commandeered the spotlight. "I've been getting used and abused for years," Kidman said, "and I'm not going to take it anymore." Kidman went on to explain to the fans in the building and those watching on TV that he was tired of being bad-mouthed by Hogan and the other veteran wrestlers. Then he called Hogan to the ring for a fight.

Calling out the Hulkster was no insignificant gesture by Kidman. Hogan stood 6' 8", weighed 275 pounds, and was the dominant wrestler of the previous two decades. Kidman, a mere 5' 11" and 195 pounds, had never won a major title. The 26-year-old Kidman challenging the veteran Hogan was like a college basketball player challenging Michael Jordan to a game of one-on-one basketball.

WCW executive vice president Eric Bischoff, center, sits with Mike Tenney, left, and Bobby Heenan, right, during a Monday Nitro *broadcast. Bischoff helped the young rising stars or "New Blood" of WCW to take the spotlight from the fedration's older, more established wrestlers.*

Hogan, never one to back down from any challenge, marched to the ring and confronted Kidman. "Stop your whining," he told Kidman. But when Hogan made a nasty comment about Torrie Wilson, Kidman's girlfriend and valet, Kidman stopped talking and started fighting. He floored Hogan with a series of kicks and punches. The battle spilled onto the arena floor, where Hogan slammed Kidman shoulder-first into the ringpost, then tossed him back into the ring. Brandishing a steel chair, Bischoff boldly made his way to the ring and told Hogan to pick up Kidman.

The moment of truth had arrived: Were the statements made by Bischoff and Russo a ruse? Had they been on the old guard's side all along? Had they merely been paying lip service to the younger WCW wrestlers?

Hogan lifted Kidman into the air . . . and Bischoff snuck up behind the Hulkster and cracked him over the head with the chair.

The crowd at The Pepsi Center in Denver, Colorado, couldn't believe what it was seeing. Fans watching at home on television were equally stunned. Blood dripped down Hogan's forehead. A stunned Hulkster collapsed to the mat. Kidman, at first shocked by what had happened, seized the opportunity to make this the greatest night of his life. He dropped his body on top of Hogan's and covered him for the pin. Bischoff made a three-count. Sure, this wasn't an official match, but for wrestling fans around the United States, the sight of Kidman covering Hogan in the middle of the ring meant only one thing: WCW's new era had arrived.

After recovering from the ambush, Hogan spent the rest of the night searching the building for Bischoff and Kidman. He looked in the dressing rooms, but couldn't find them. He looked in the skyboxes, but couldn't find them. Frustrated by his failure to find Bischoff and Kidman, Hogan got into his limousine and prepared to leave the building. While Hogan spoke on the phone to his lawyer, a white Hummer sped toward the limousine. Hogan stared helplessly as the car closed in on him. The Hummer smashed into the side of Hogan's limo, backed up, then smashed it again. And again. And again.

When the damage was done, Kidman and Bischoff emerged from the Hummer.

But the humiliation wasn't complete. As medical personnel strapped Hogan to a stretcher and prepared to take him to the hospital, Bischoff and Kidman reappeared on the scene and spray-painted three initials on Hogan's chest.

TNB. The New Blood.

Kidman's career had received the transfusion it so desperately needed.

2

LIVING HERE
IN ALLENTOWN

The man the wrestling world came to know as Billy Kidman was born Pete Gruner on May 11, 1974, in Allentown, Pennsylvania. Allentown, a midsize city in eastern Pennsylvania, isn't known for much. Billy Joel wrote a song called "Allentown," but that is about the extent of what most people know of the city.

Knowledgeable wrestling fans know about Allentown, though, because it has always been a great place for wrestling. In the 1970s, the WWF held its monthly TV tapings there. Independent federations frequently hold cards there, too. Former WCW World tag team champions the Nasty Boys are natives of Allentown. The big-time spotlight of the WWF and WCW frequently shines in Philadelphia, only 60 miles away.

For a kid who dreamed of becoming a professional wrestler, Allentown wasn't a bad place to be, and like most wrestling fans who grew up in the 1980s, Pete Gruner loved and admired the star who led wrestling's explosion of popularity in that decade: Hulk Hogan.

"He was the man back then," Kidman recalled in an interview with *WOW Magazine*. "I was a typical [fan] who loved all the babyfaces [good guys] and hated all the heels [bad guys].

All the wrestlers Pete Gruner grew up watching on television were huge like Andre the Giant, Jake "the Snake" Roberts, Randy "Macho Man" Savage, and Hulk Hogan. Even though he stopped growing at a mere 5' 11", Gruner didn't let his size stop him from pursuing his dream of becoming a professional wrestler.

I saw him one time in person at the Hartford Civic Center the day after a Survivor Series. It was the first live show I ever saw. My father took me to it. I didn't care who was there, I was just happy to see a live show."

While watching that show, Gruner must have noticed how big the wrestlers were. Hogan was 6' 8", 275 pounds. Other WWF stars of that era, such as the Ultimate Warrior, Jake Roberts, Andre the Giant, Big Bossman, and Randy Savage were all in excess of six feet tall and 230 pounds.

Gruner? He stopped growing at 5' 11", 195 pounds.

But Gruner was always extremely athletic, and he kept himself busy playing sports throughout his teenage years. From Kernsville Elementary to Troxell Junior High to Parkland High, Kidman was a standout in baseball and track. Wrestling, however, was his first love and his total obsession, and his favorite wrestlers were the ones who could both fly through the air and grapple on the mat. His hero was Ricky "the Dragon" Steamboat—the remarkable athletic star who was as great a scientific grappler as he was an aerial artist. Steamboat won the WWF Intercontinental title in 1987 and the WCW World heavyweight title in 1989.

Fortunately for Gruner, Allentown was the new home of Afa's Wild Samoan Wrestling Training Center. Samoan Afa was a three-time WWF World tag team champion in the early 1980s. He had trained superstars such as Paul Orndorff, Junkyard Dog, Michael Hayes, Luna Vachon, Hulk Hogan, and Brutus Beefcake at his training center in Pensacola, Florida. Yokozuna, the Headshrinkers, and

Pete Gruner knew he was not the largest of wrestlers, but he had enough attitude and energy— not to mention aerial skills—to make up for it.

Sherri Martel trained at his training center in Connecticut. In the late 1980s, Afa opened a training center in Allentown.

"I was 16 years old and I would go to the Wild Samoan Training Center and watch them train," Kidman recalled. "It was always a dream for me, but Afa wouldn't let me train." Indeed, the veteran star was clear in his response: "Come back when you're 18," Afa told Gruner, who did as he was told. Two years later, Gruner again came knocking at the door of the Wild Samoan Training Center.

"After a while, he spent so much time here that I figured I might as well train him," Afa told *The Wrestler* magazine. "He always had a lot of heart and natural ability, even though he isn't big. But heart and ability can make up for that."

Gruner borrowed money from his college tuition fund and worked a wide variety of odd jobs to pay for wrestling school. He was intent on doing everything in his power to become a professional wrestler—even though, unlike Afa, his role models, and most of the others who were training with him, he didn't have a lot of size or power.

At age 18 Pete Gruner began training at Samoan Afa's Wild Samoan Training Center in Allentown, Pennsylvania. Afa, who has trained many professional wrestlers, taught Pete to use his small size to his advantage and to rely on his wits in order to handle the bigger wrestlers.

"Most of the guys at that school were a lot bigger than me, but none of them had more determination or athletic ability," he recalled. "There were times when I'd get thrown around the ring, so I realized I had to be smarter, quicker, and more athletic than the bigger wrestlers. The bigger guys can win on size and strength alone. I have to rely on ability and intelligence. I found that out the hard way, by taking a lot of bumps."

Gruner spent most of his time honing his aerial skills. From the start, he was a fearless daredevil. He developed outstanding dropkicks, including what he called a "missile dropkick" from the ropes, and a spectacular variation of the moonsault which would one day be known as the shooting star press. When executing the shooting star press, Gruner stands on the ropes or on the mat in front of his downed victim. Then he jumps and performs a backflip before landing on his victim. The move is difficult to pull off, because it requires the attacker to jump forward and do a backflip at the same time.

By the time Gruner was ready to make his professional debut in 1994, Afa had no doubt that his pupil had enough determination and ability to match any wrestler in the world.

But one question remained: Could little Pete Gruner survive in the land of the giants?

3 FROM KID FLASH TO THE FLOCK

It would be nice to be able to say that Pete Gruner was an instant star in professional wrestling. Unfortunately, he wasn't.

There's no shame in that, of course. Most wrestlers aren't a big national sensation when they first arrive on the wrestling scene. Everyone remembers that athletes such as Lex Luger, Bill Goldberg, and Sting were proverbial overnight successes, but they're the exception rather than the rule. Even "Stone Cold" Steve Austin, who became the biggest superstar in wrestling history, toiled in anonymity for years before getting his big break in the WWF.

Most successful professional wrestlers start like Gruner did: at the bottom.

Gruner's first wrestling name was Kid Flash. He made his pro debut in the fall of 1994 at a small wrestling show in Reading, Pennsylvania. It wasn't the best of starts: Kid Flash lost to an unknown named "Disco" Joey Travolla.

Kid Flash spent the rest of 1994 and all of 1995 wrestling throughout New Jersey and Pennsylvania in small independent promotions such as the East Coast Wrestling Alliance (ECWA), the American Wrestling Federation (AWF), and the Trans World Wrestling Federation (TWWF). After that first

---

Gruner wrestled in several small promotions before making it to WCW, where his talent and his efforts to promote himself finally began to pay off.

loss, things turned around for him in a hurry. He went on to win his first singles championship, the TWWF junior heavyweight title, and his first tag team championship, the ECWA tag team title with partner Ace Darling. The relationship with Darling, however, quickly soured after they lost the ECWA tag team belts to Steve Corino and Lance Diamond. Darling blamed Kid Flash for the loss.

"I can't tell you how many veteran wrestlers have told me they can't count how many friends they've had that turned into enemies," Kid Flash said after his first experience with a friend becoming an enemy. "That's one thing Afa told me: 'Never get too close to anybody, because in this sport, it's dog eat dog.' I try to remember that, but at some point, you have to trust *somebody*."

But who would that somebody be? Kid Flash teamed with Corey Student to beat Darling and Gino Caruso on an NWA card in Tower City, Pennsylvania, on October 14, 1995, but their partnership was short-lived, too.

The one thing Kidman did have was a lot of friends and admirers in the wrestling business. Among his mentors at Afa's wrestling school were Chris Kanyon and Terry Taylor, both of whom saw in Kidman the necessary desire and skill to make it in wrestling . . . if only he got a few key breaks.

"He's like a million other kids who have dreams and want to make it," Taylor said at the time. "He has great talent, but it comes down to how much he wants it. The real tests have yet to come."

Would Pete Gruner be just another one of a million? Or would he become that rare one in a million? Kid Flash never stopped shooting for the stars, even while he was about as low as he could get in wrestling.

"The dream is to one day be recognized as the greatest aerial wrestler in the world and to win a world championship," he told *The Wrestler*. "I'm just trying to take it slow, and I'm doing what people tell me to do. I'm in good hands, and I love what I'm doing."

Unfortunately, when Kid Flash said he was going to take it slow, he had no idea how slow, painstaking, and time-consuming the job of becoming a well-known wrestler would be. As Taylor said, there are millions of other people who have the same dream. The independent ranks of professional wrestling are jam-packed with wrestlers who will never in their lives wrestle in front of crowds of more than a few hundred people.

And don't forget, at 5' 11", Kid Flash wasn't exactly the kind of guy who stood out in a crowd, much less a crowd of professional wrestlers.

Fortunately for Kid Flash, though, wrestling was undergoing a change in the mid-1990s. Although size was still important, a lack of size didn't necessarily prevent a man from becoming a successful pro wrestler, as long as he had real ability.

The WCW cruiserweight title, which had lain dormant since 1992, was once again in contention. On March 20, 1996, Shinjiro Otani beat Chris Benoit in the final round of a tournament to win that vacant championship. Over the following months, cruiserweights such as Dean Malenko, Rey Misterio Jr., and Ultimo Dragon actively pursued the title. Wrestling fans couldn't help but notice that these little guys were the most talented and exciting wrestlers around. While the big guys lumbered around the ring and pounded each other with fists, elbows, and kicks, the little guys soared and took chances. The action was always non-stop in cruiserweight matches.

"It would have been much harder if cruiser-weights had not made their way to the United States," Gruner said in an Internet interview. "When Chris Kanyon, who helped train me along with Afa, told me to send in a tape [to WCW], I never really did it. Then he said they were bringing in Rey Misterio Jr., who is smaller than me, and they were going to do the cruiserweight division. I put the tape together and sent it in, and that's what got me in."

In June 1996, Pete Gruner arrived in WCW with a new name: Billy Kidman.

At this point, Kidman had every reason to believe that he was about to become a big star in professional wrestling. He believed in him-self. He felt that nobody could match his aerial skills. After two years of toiling in the minor leagues, he finally had his big break . . . or so it seemed.

In reality, frustration was about to build upon frustration for Kidman. He had gone from being a big fish in some very small ponds to being the smallest fish in the biggest pond of all. Kidman's arrival in WCW wasn't heralded by press conferences and massive media cover-age. The truth was, Kidman's arrival in WCW wasn't heralded at all.

Kidman was no Bill Goldberg, who made a much different entrance to WCW. The 6' 4", 285-pound former college football star with the

massive muscles and intimidating stare started
out at the bottom, just as Kidman had done.
But when Goldberg dominated and won his
first match, he got another one the next
night, and then another one the night after
that. Within a year, Goldberg has amassed a
173-match winning streak and had become
a WCW superstar.

That's what happens when you're a big
man.

When you're Billy Kidman, though, you
don't even wrestle 173 matches in a year, much

*Unlike Bill Goldberg,
who was an instant
sensation in WCW,
Billy Kidman had
to work his way up
from the bottom of
the federation.*

less win them all. In his first year in WCW, in fact, Kidman barely wrestled 50 times. He usually lost.

Kidman made his *WCW Monday Nitro* debut on June 10, 1996, and lost to Steven Regal. In August, famed Mexican wrestler Juventud Guerrera made his WCW debut on *Nitro*—against Kidman. This figured to be a great test for Kidman. Juventud was only 5' 5", 165 pounds, but, like Kidman, he was an outstanding aerial and mat wrestler. Kidman lost this bout, too. The problem was not only that Kidman wasn't getting many matches, he wasn't even winning the ones he was getting.

On August 20, 1996, Kidman lost to "Diamond" Dallas Page in Dalton, Georgia. At the time, Page wasn't the superstar he would become, and the match was just another in a series of undistinguished losses for Kidman.

Over the next several months, Kidman wrestled in opening matches at nontelevised arena cards, never wrestled on pay-per-view cards, and got his only TV attention on *WCW Saturday Night*, which had a tiny audience compared to the audiences for *Nitro* and *Thunder*.

When Kidman got his breaks, he didn't make the most of them. At the December 2, 1996, *Nitro*, Kidman got a shot at cruiserweight champion Dean Malenko. Kidman lost when he submitted to Malenko. A few nights later, Kidman lost to Malenko again.

Even though Kidman lost the matches to Malenko, the opportunities should have served as some kind of career springboard. They didn't. Over the following months, he lost to midcard wrestlers such as Scotty Riggs, Glacier, and Disco Inferno. In March 1997, he lost again

As he struggled to promote himself, one of Kidman's most promising matches was against Rey Misterio, Jr. Wrestling fans enjoyed watching the two cruiserweights battle in a nonstop match. High-flying aerial moves and action-packed matches helped to popularize the cruiserweight division of WCW in the 1990s.

to Page, who had by then moved up to number six in the *Pro Wrestling Illustrated* ratings.

Kidman scored an important win on March 15, 1997, in Florence, South Carolina. He beat U.S. champion Eddy Guerrero by countout. Unfortunately for Kidman, the title could only change hands on a pinfall or submission. Kidman returned to the bottom of the WCW roster and kept losing matches to competitors

Though Kidman faced "Diamond" Dallas Page in a 1996 WCW match and lost, Page was not a federation headliner at the time and the match did not further Kidman's career.

such as Alex Wright, Greg Valentine, and Hector Guerrero. A sensational match against 5' 3", 140-pound cruiserweight Rey Misterio Jr. ended with Misterio pinning Kidman.

It was difficult at times, but Kidman tried not to get down on himself. In fact, if he looked closely, he could see that his career was actually headed in the right direction. He was wrestling more often. He appeared on *WCW Saturday Night* almost every week. He was facing better opponents. Sure, he was losing most of his matches, but he was honing his skills against a wide variety of opponents. Best of all, people were starting to notice him.

On October 4, 1997, Kidman scored one of the most important victories of his career when he pinned Alex Wright on *WCW Saturday Night.* Wright was certainly no superstar, but he was well known by all fans and had held the WCW cruiserweight title for three weeks earlier that year. Fans and WCW promoters took notice. So did a man named Raven.

Raven, a two-time Extreme Championship Wrestling (ECW) heavyweight champion in 1996, had recently arrived in WCW and was looking for a way to make people notice him. Raven was a rough-and-tumble wrestler who was no stranger to rulebreaking, and his idea was to form a clique that would run roughshod over WCW.

On October 6, 1997, Raven and Perry Saturn watched at ringside as Wright defeated Kidman in a rematch. A few days later, Raven and Saturn met with Kidman and talked him into becoming a member of The Flock. A week later, a new Billy Kidman arrived in WCW.

The old Billy Kidman was clean-cut and never broke the rules. He had respect for the fans, even though they didn't have much respect for him, and was outgoing in interviews.

The new Billy Kidman sported the dirty grunge look. He had long hair and rarely shaved. The dark side of Kidman surfaced. He rarely said much in interviews, allowing Raven to do the talking for him. Raven was the leader of The Flock. Kidman, Saturn, Reese, Lodi, and Scotty Riggs were his followers.

It would be too easy to judge Kidman and say he sold out, or that he sold out his values and gave in to a man who didn't have his best interests at heart. Perhaps those criticisms would even be correct, but they would fail to take into account the truth about Kidman's first three years in the sport: despite his talent, nobody was noticing him.

Joining The Flock got Kidman what he wanted at that point in his career: It got him noticed.

Unfortunately, it didn't get him noticed for his ability. It got him noticed for his willingness to interfere in matches involving Raven and other members of The Flock. Shortly after joining The Flock, Kidman lost to cruiserweight champion Rey Misterio Jr. A month later, he lost to Chris Benoit at *Nitro*.

Finally, in February 1998, fans started noticing Kidman for his wrestling ability when he lost a spectacular match against Ultimo Dragon. The match was considered by some to be one of the best of the year. Three days later, Kidman scored his biggest WCW victory by using his shooting star press to pin Juventud Guerrera.

Suddenly, Kidman became a central figure on major WCW TV events. He again used the shooting star press to pin top cruiserweight Prince Iaukea. He got more matches and piled up more wins. Losses to Ultimo Dragon and Juventud didn't stop Kidman, who was gaining confidence with each bout. Even a loss to Dean Malenko in a spectacular battle of skills enhanced Kidman's reputation.

The matches against Juventud were classics, too. Kidman and Juventud wrestled three times in one month, with Juventud winning twice. On July 12, 1998, Kidman made his WCW pay-per-view debut by wrestling Guerrera at Bash at the Beach in a match that had fans talking for weeks afterward. Guerrera and Kidman's nonstop, all-out, daring style featured innova-tive moves and seemingly endless strings of aerial maneuvers. It got everybody's attention. When Guerrera regained the cruiserweight title on August 8, 1998, Kidman received one of the first title shots.

But problems within The Flock were over-shadowing Kidman's career progress. The group was in turmoil. Many members, including Kidman, felt they were sacrificing their careers for Raven's benefit. For example, at Spring Stampede '98, interference by The Flock helped Raven beat Dallas Page for the U.S. heavy-weight title. The other members of The Flock had to ask themselves, "What are we getting out of this?"

Kidman couldn't answer that question by saying, "Nothing." Even he had to admit that his career had taken off after joining Raven's brood. And there was another problem. Raven had brainwashed the members of The Flock, including Kidman. Only one man was free from Raven's control: Perry Saturn.

Raven and Saturn feuded over control of The Flock throughout the summer of 1998. Finally, at Fall Brawl on September 13, Saturn battled Raven. If Saturn won, The Flock would be freed. If Raven won, Saturn would rejoin The Flock, which would remain under Raven's control. Late in the match, after Lodi, Horace Boulder, and Sick Boy had all interfered, Kidman bounded into the ring and hit Raven with a missile dropkick. Saturn covered Raven for the pin. The Flock was free. Kidman was free.

The next day, a clean-cut and much more outgoing Kidman showed up at *Nitro* and beat Juventud Guerrera for his first WCW cruiser-weight title.

Kidman's career had taken a major turn for the better.

Raven convinced Kidman to join his Flock, so Kidman transformed himself from a clean-cut good guy to a grungy slacker.

4 THE CRUISERWEIGHTS

By some measures, Billy Kidman's long, hard road to the top wasn't really that long or that hard. When he won the WCW cruiserweight title, he was 24 years old. Six years had passed since he started taking wrestling lessons from Afa. Four years had passed since he first stepped into the ring professionally. Only a year and a half had passed since he signed with WCW.

But those years seemed hard and long to Kidman because progress had come so slowly during most of them. He had time to prepare for success. When it finally arrived, he was ready to meet it.

Kidman racked up one successful title defense after another. In his first defense, which took place on September 21, 1998, he beat Disco Inferno. Although he lost to Scott Hall in a non-title match (Hall, at 6' 8" and 290 pounds, is far from being a cruiserweight), he bounced back from that loss to upend Psicosis in the first of many matches between the two. On October 19, Kidman and Misterio battled to a spectacular time-limit draw at *WCW Monday Nitro*. A title defense at Halloween Havoc '98 saw Kidman beat Disco Inferno again.

The cruiserweights were stealing the show, and Kidman was ruling the cruiserweights. With the cruiserweight title

---

A month after earning his first WCW World cruiserweight title, Billy Kidman lost the championship to Juventud Guerrera, then won it back again six days later.

firmly in hand, Kidman boldly took a run at a heavyweight title: the WCW TV championship held by Chris Jericho. Kidman battled this outstanding scientific wrestler to a time-limit draw. He didn't win the title, but he again added to his reputation as a talented all-around wrestler.

Finally, on November 16, 1998, Kidman lost the cruiserweight title to Juventud Guerrera. His down time didn't last long. Six days later at the World War III pay-per-view in Auburn Hills, Michigan, Kidman was given a chance to regain the championship. Juventud appeared headed to victory as he was about to attempt his huracanrana, a maneuver in which Guerrera catapults his foe into the ropes, leaps into the air, extends his legs in front of him, wraps his legs around his opponent's head, then arches his body back and swings himself underneath his foe and through his opponent's legs, rolling his foe into a tight pin attempt. Before the move was able to be executed, Rey Misterio Jr. interfered, costing Guerrera the match. Kidman won his second cruiserweight title.

"I guess I'm supposed to thank Rey, but I won't," said Kidman, who wasn't happy with how he won. "I'm not sure he even deserves a shot at my title."

Kidman had every reason not to trust Misterio. The California-born *luchador* was a member of the Latin World Order (LWO), which also included Eddy Guerrero and Guerrera. Misterio, however, didn't want to be a member of the group anymore, so in late November 1998, Guerrero and Guerrera cost Misterio his match against Kidman. A week later, Misterio's interference cost Guerrero his match against Kidman.

The cruiserweight division had become the most exciting aspect of WCW. In past years, fans might have used a match between light-weights as a chance to grab a snack from their refrigerators. Now, fans were staying in their seats for the cruiserweight matches . . . at least until the matches started. After that, they'd be up and screaming for their favorites. At the time, no cruiserweight was more popular than Kidman.

Kidman made the ultimate defense of his title at Starrcade '98 on December 27. Starrcade has traditionally been the most important pay-per-view of WCW's year, the organization's equivalent of the WWF's WrestleMania. For Kidman, it would become the most important night of his life. He defended the title against Juventud Guerrera and Rey Misterio Jr., both former champions, in a triple threat match. Kidman faced the risk of losing his title if was pinned by either man.

The match was a clinic in aerial artistry. Guerrera nailed Misterio with a top-rope Frankensteiner (a move that is similar to the huracanrana, except it's designed to drive the recipient's head into the mat rather than roll him up for the pin) while Misterio was perched on Kidman's shoulders. Later, Misterio dropped both men to ringside with a moonsault. Kidman responded with a shooting star press to the outside of the ring. All three wrestlers scored several near-falls on each other, but Kidman pinned Guerrera while Misterio held off Eddy Guerrero, who was trying to interfere. But Kidman's night wasn't over. He came out again and wrestled Guerrero in another title match. Kidman pinned Guerrero to retain the belt.

Kidman struggles to pin Juventud Guerrera and the ref prepares to make the three-count.

"I think that was the night when the fans finally took notice, especially when I had to come out afterwards and wrestle again," Kidman said in an Internet interview. "Career-wise, or pay-per-view-wise, that was probably my best match."

The tests got tougher for Kidman. As if a triple threat match wasn't enough of a challenge, Kidman squared off against Juventud, Misterio, and Psicosis in a quadruple threat match at Souled Out on January 17, 1999. Again, Kidman pinned Juventud to retain the belt.

Challenges to Kidman's title came from all over. He beat Juventud and Misterio in another three-way match. In February 1999, WCW new-comer Lash Laroux gave Kidman all he could handle. Laroux proved just as nimble as the champion, wowing viewers with several sharp huracanranas, and matching Kidman step for step. Kidman eventually got the win after connecting with the shooting star press. At SuperBrawl IX, Kidman pinned Chavo Guerrero Jr. At *Nitro*, he used his shooting star press to pin Psicosis.

Kidman and the other cruiserweights had a way of stealing the show from the bigger wrestlers. Ric Flair vs. Hulk Hogan was the main event of Uncensored on March 14, 1999, in Louisville, Kentucky, but Kidman vs. former ECW star Mikey Whipwreck was the match viewers would remember. Kidman won the bout with a shooting star press after Whipwreck countered many of Kidman's moves that, up to that point, had seemed impossible to counter. The fans were on their feet throughout the bout, which was by far the best match on the card.

Perhaps that grueling evening took its toll on Kidman. The following night at *Nitro*, Kidman's four-month reign as champion ended when he was pinned by Misterio.

Kidman and Misterio had an unusual relationship. They had been partners in the war against the now-defunct LWO. Misterio had been one of the wrestlers in several of Kidman's triple threat match defenses. Misterio won the title from Kidman. And they would form a successful tag team: On March 29, 1999, Kidman and Misterio made an impact in WCW's tag team division by beating Chris Benoit and Dean Malenko for the WCW World tag team title.

Kidman and Misterio were still tag team champions when they battled one-on-one for the cruiserweight title at Spring Stampede on April 11. Misterio hit his head on the stairs leading to the ring, but recovered to score the pin in a hotly contested match that saw the advantage change hands several times.

Many people thought it was merely a matter of time before Kidman and Misterio were at each other's throats. One night at *Nitro*, Misterio got angry at Kidman for not saving him from an attack by Malenko and Benoit. Kidman apologized, saying he had been making a promotional appearance for WCW and had just arrived at the arena, but it was hard to ignore the implications of what might really have happened. Perhaps Kidman was happy that Benoit and Malenko were weakening the cruiserweight champion.

The relationship between Kidman and Misterio resulted in some unusual occurrences. One night in Baltimore, they were wrestling for the cruiserweight title when Benoit and Malenko showed up at ringside and demanded a tag team title match. Misterio and Kidman accepted, turning a singles match into a tag team title defense.

"It was strange," Kidman told *Pro Wrestling Illustrated* magazine. "I don't think I've ever had anything like that happen to me. One second I want to beat the man, the next second I'm on his side. It takes a big adjustment in your mindset to get used to something like that, but fortunately we got through it with the belts around our waists."

Kidman and Misterio won the match when Kidman pinned Malenko, yet the question persisted: Could Misterio and Kidman remain friends?

"I don't know," Misterio said. "It's worth trying. I don't know. I didn't like it when Billy didn't save me from that attack by Malenko and Benoit, but I accepted his excuse. I have to. He's my partner."

On May 9, 1999, Kidman and Misterio were able to stop worrying about the tag team title. They lost the belts to Perry Saturn and Raven in a three-way match that also involved Malenko and Benoit. Meanwhile, Misterio had lost and regained the cruiserweight title from Psicosis.

Somehow, the friendship between Kidman and Misterio survived. Perhaps it had to do with the enormous respect these two men hold for

Kidman jumps off the ropes and hurtles toward Eddie Guerrero, below, while Rey Misterio watches from outside the ring. Kidman pinned Guerrero in the match and retained his cruiserweight title.

each other. A match between Misterio and Kidman wasn't about hurting each other and inflicting pain, it was about skill and mutual excellence. Kidman and Misterio enjoyed wrestling each other because each match forced them to invent new moves and become better wrestlers.

"Rey's had a lot to do with how much I've improved over the past year," Kidman admitted.

While Kidman's most formidable opponent was perhaps his closest friend, he nonetheless had no shortage of enemies. In mid-1999, 230-pound heavyweight Hugh Morris set out to destroy every WCW cruiserweight. Morris interfered in a 12-man cruiserweight battle royal and eliminated nearly every contestant. Kidman won the match by eliminating Juventud Guerrera. Over the next few weeks, Kidman scored two impressive victories over Morris, who had the size, but not the skill, to deal with Billy.

The feud with Morris opened a new era in Kidman's career. For years, he had fought mostly fellow cruiserweights. Beginning in the summer of 1999, he started taking on the big guys, including a match against "Macho Man" Randy Savage at *Nitro*.

There were many instances of interference. A match between Kidman and Misterio for the cruiserweight title ended when heavyweights Curt Hennig and Bobby Duncum of the West Texas Rednecks interfered. Vampiro interfered in a match between Kidman and Guerrero at *Thunder*. Enough was enough. At that point, the cruiserweights decided to bond as a group: Kidman, Misterio, Guerrero, and Konnan formed the Filthy Animals.

When Kidman was a member of Raven's Flock, the wrestling world was introduced to his dark side. As a member of the Filthy Animals, Kidman showed off his playful side. At *Nitro* on August 16, 1999, Kidman was being interviewed by Gene Okerlund when he admitted that he was attracted to Kimberly Page. Kidman's comment infuriated "Diamond" Dallas Page, Kimberly's husband, and resulted in an impromptu match. Kidman's subsequent victory over the former WCW World heavyweight champion was among the most impressive of his career.

The Filthy Animals never backed down from a feud. They battled with Perry Saturn's Revolution. Kidman and Misterio feuded with Juventud Guerrera and Psicosis.

When Kidman tried to unmask Psicosis, Chavo Guerrero came to Psicosis's rescue. Then Chavo challenged Kidman to take on Psicosis in a hair vs. mask match. Kidman accepted. Kidman won the match the following week at *Nitro* and tore off Psicosis's mask.

Meanwhile, Kidman was never afraid of angering an opponent, and he started gaining a reputation as a man with an eye for other men's wives and girlfriends. In October, Kidman and Torrie Wilson, David Flair's beautiful valet, appeared to be flirting with each other. There was ample evidence to believe this was true. For example, Torrie's lipstick was seen on Kidman's cheek. David Flair confronted his valet with the evidence, but Torrie said his accusations were ridiculous. A week later, Kidman bought Torrie a mink coat.

Flair's suspicions were confirmed in brutal fashion at the October 18, 1999, *Nitro* when he

Torrie Wilson was dating David Flair when she met Billy Kidman, but she quickly dropped Flair to be with Kidman and even went so far as to help Billy defeat her ex-boyfriend in the ring.

battled Kidman. Before the match, David got enraged as Torrie and Kidman flirted. The match ended when Torrie distracted Flair, enabling Kidman to win with the shooting star press. The Filthy Animals stormed the ring and attacked Flair. From that point on, Kidman and Torrie were officially an item.

The next *Nitro* was a big one for Kidman. First, thanks to interference from Harlem Heat, he beat Konnan in the first round of a tournament for the vacant WCW World title. Then he and Konnan teamed to battle Harlem Heat for the WCW World tag team title. Here was a situation similar to the one Kidman had faced earlier in the year: wrestling against a friend, then teaming with him later in the night. Kidman and Konnan beat the Heat to win the belts, but the night ended on a disturbing note as Torrie was kidnapped by the Revolution.

Every week at *Nitro*, Kidman was in the middle of the action. On November 1, Eddie Guerrero rescued Torrie from the Revolution. Later in the night, Kidman and Konnan successfully defended the tag belts against Sting and Lex Luger, attacking Sting after the match. On November 8, Kidman advanced to the quarterfinals of the world title tournament. His world title dream ended the following week, though, when he lost to Bret Hart.

The year ended on a down note for Kidman. On November 22, 1999, Creative Control—the team of Ron and Don Harris formed by WCW writer Vince Russo—defeated Kidman and Konnan for the belts. Kidman and Guerrero started to feud over Torrie Wilson. At the last *Nitro* of 1999, Kidman not only lost to Jeff Jarrett, but the Filthy Animals were annihilated by Scott Hall and Kevin Nash of the New World Order (NWO). Clearly, the Filthy Animals's days were numbered.

Overall though, 1999 had been a great year for Kidman, his first full year as a WCW superstar. In 1998, Kidman had been ranked No. 132 in *Pro Wrestling Illustrated*'s ranking of the top 500 wrestlers of the year. In the 1999 edition, he shot up to No. 31.

Without a doubt, Billy Kidman had finally arrived.

THE NEW BLOOD

WCW was on a downswing when the new millennium opened. Every Monday night, the federation suffered the humiliation of getting trounced in the television ratings war between *Nitro* and the WWF's *Monday Night Raw*.

Attendance was down. Pay-per-view buy rates were down. Television ratings were down. Every week, the Rock, Triple-H, and the Giant, the hot young stars of the WWF, would do something outlandish and exciting to capture viewers' attention. And each week, the few loyal WCW viewers remaining would complain that they were tired of seeing Hulk Hogan, Ric Flair, Sting, "Diamond" Dallas Page, Lex Luger, Terry Funk, and the other veteran stars dominating *Nitro*. Where, they asked, was WCW's young blood?

"Here I am!" Billy Kidman could have answered. And while it was true that Kidman was getting many more chances now than he was a year ago, he still wasn't regarded as a main-event star. He hadn't even wrestled at Starrcade '99, the latest version of WCW's oldest and most important pay-per-view event.

Kidman started 2000 with a bang. After getting shut out of Starrcade, he wrestled three times at Souled Out on January 17. He beat Dean Malenko and Perry Saturn, but lost to Chris

With Torrie at his side, Billy Kidman's popularity in WCW soared, and he began piling up victory after victory over the superstars of the federation.

Former WCW World tag team champion Booker T of Harlem Heat teamed with Kidman briefly, but the tag team belt eluded them.

Benoit. One night later at *Nitro*, Kidman kicked out after Psicosis scored with a legdrop and rallied to score the pin.

Earlier in the month, Kidman threatened to leave WCW and jump to another federation. He was concerned that he wasn't getting a big enough push from WCW promoters and writers. He decided to stay after WCW officials promised him a larger role, but the Filthy Animals were falling apart. Eddy Guerrero had jumped to the WWF. Rey Misterio Jr. was nursing an ankle injury. Konnan had been suspended. Kidman had nobody, except, of course, the beautiful Torrie Wilson.

For a while, that proved to be enough. Torrie's interference helped Kidman survive a month-long feud with Vampiro that ended with a spectacular victory at SuperBrawl 2000. After the Harris Boys interfered in a match between Kidman and heavyweight Booker T, the two former world tag team champions formed a shaky alliance and went after the tag team belts. They got their first shot at the March 20 *Nitro* in a match against the Harris brothers. Booker T, a 10-time former tag team champion, manhandled the Harris Brothers early in the match, but Ron Harris hit Booker T with the title belt and got his team disqualified.

Unfortunately for Kidman, he and Booker T never won the tag team belts. Fortunately for Kidman, his career was about to soar.

On April 10, 2000, WCW executives Eric Bischoff and Vince Russo introduced a new era in WCW. Kidman called out Hulk Hogan for a fight, and pinned the legendary Hulkster in the middle of the ring.

"It was probably the highlight of my career so far," Kidman said of the match against Hogan.

The lines had been drawn in WCW between the New Blood and the Millionaires Club, and more specifically between Kidman and Hogan.

Six days later at Spring Stampede, Kidman lost to Vampiro in the first round of the U.S. title tournament when Hogan interfered and beat up Kidman. The next night at *Nitro*, Hogan was again after Kidman.

Kidman vs. Hogan became a regular event at *Nitro*. On April 24, Kidman and former ECW heavyweight champion Mike Awesome battled Hogan in a handicap match. Hogan suffered a brutal beating at the hands of the New Blood, and Kidman pinned Hogan following a legdrop. Kidman and Awesome powerbombed Hogan through a table. Kevin Nash tried to save Hogan, but Kidman and Awesome bashed him with a chair.

The war between the New Blood and the Millionaires Club was actually the playing out of a debate that had raged among WCW fans for several years: Should WCW nurture its young talent, or should it continue to rely on the veterans who had carried it to the top of the ratings war in the mid-1990s? Many fans thought the New Blood wrestlers weren't ready to carry the federation. Others felt, considering how poorly WCW was doing in the ratings, nothing would be lost in giving them the chance to have their day in the spotlight.

The wrestlers were fighting for their careers. Kidman and the other New Blood members wanted to become WCW superstars. Hogan, Flair, Sting, and the other Millionaires Club members were trying to protect their turf.

Hogan was the main target of the New Blood. Kidman interfered in a match between Awesome and Hogan and busted open Hogan's head with a chair. Awesome covered Hogan for the pin.

Although Kidman continued taking on the biggest stars in the sport, he couldn't move closer to his ultimate goal of winning the WCW World heavyweight title. He was one of the last four contestants remaining in a battle royal for a world title shot, but got eliminated by Hogan. Bischoff was the guest referee for a match between Hogan and Kidman at Slamboree 2000, but that didn't prevent Hogan from pinning Kidman, thanks to interference by the Hulkster's nephew Horace Hogan.

Nitro on May 8, 2000, marked the official return of the Filthy Animals. Nash called out Russo, but Kidman, Torrie, Konnan, and Misterio Jr. came out instead.

"The Filthy Animals are back, and you'd better be ready," Konnan warned Nash.

The Millionaire's Club members didn't know who to trust. One night, Hulk Hogan and Billy Kidman battled in a three-way match that also involved Horace Hogan. Horace stood and watched as Hogan worked over Kidman, but then the Filthy Animals stormed the ring. The two Hogans cleaned house, then Torrie Wilson walked to the ring. Horace nodded to Torrie, then clobbered his uncle with a chair. Now the Hulkster's own nephew was a member of the New Blood.

But Kidman, who had stolen Torrie from David Flair, had reason to think Torrie might be involved with Horace. This resulted in a match at *Nitro* between Horace and Kidman—with Torrie as the special referee. During the match, Hogan interfered and slammed Kidman on top of Horace and through a table. Hogan demanded that Torrie make the three-count, and she complied reluctantly.

Horace Hogan was the guest referee for the battle between the Hulkster and Kidman at the 2000 Great American Bash. Although Kidman desperately wanted to beat Hogan, Hulk had far more on the line. He had vowed to retire if he lost. If he won, he would get a shot at the WCW World heavyweight champion.

Hulk Hogan was the posterboy for WCW's Millionaire's Club in its war with the New Blood, and the young wrestlers concentrated their assault on Hogan because he stood for all the established superstars and their efforts to monopolize the limelight of WCW.

The match was a disaster for Kidman. Torrie Wilson handed Hulk a pair of brass knuckles. Kidman intercepted them and nailed Hogan to score a two-count, but Torrie kneed Kidman below the belt. Hogan won the match, and the relationship between Torrie and Kidman was over.

The war between Hulk Hogan and Kidman, however, was just heating up. The next night, Kidman was special referee for the match between Hogan and WCW World champion Jeff Jarrett at *Nitro*. Of course, WCW officials knew this wouldn't be a fair match. There was no way Kidman would be an unbiased referee. But Kidman allowed both men to use foreign objects, such as chairs, a guardrail, and a weightlifting belt. Then, as Jarrett took control of the match, Kidman grabbed a chair and threw it to Hogan. Goldberg stormed the ring and attacked Kidman and Hogan, but G.I. Bro saved Hogan and Kidman from further harm.

The fans had to wonder: what was going on here? Their questions became more complicated when Kidman saved Lance Storm from an attack by the Filthy Animals.

Kidman and Storm teamed to defeat Misterio and Juventud Guerrera at *Thunder*, but lost to Misterio and the Juice at *Nitro*, thanks to interference by Konnan and Disco Inferno. At *Thunder* on July 5, 2000, Kidman lost a four-way match that also involved Storm, Misterio, and Disco Inferno.

The war between the Filthy Animals, past and present, had overshadowed Kidman's feud with Hogan and the other established WCW stars. Once again, Kidman was on the outside looking in as established WCW stars—and other young guns—took center stage. Jarrett won the world title. Then Nash won the world title. Then Booker T won the world title. Then Nash and Booker T won it again. Kidman was completely absent from this championship picture. Even worse, he was no longer contending for the WCW cruiserweight title.

Kidman had to wonder: Had Bischoff and Russo really ushered in a new era of WCW, or had his feud with Hogan simply been a minor scene in a show that had been playing out the same way for decades?

Outside the ring, Kidman's career had taken off. He appeared on the TV show *The Dating Game* and in the movie *Ready to Rumble*. Female fans loved him, but one woman—the woman he wanted most—didn't want to be with him anymore.

Torrie had found another man.

6 | TORRIE! TORRIE! TORRIE!

Shane Douglas was no stranger to longtime wrestling fans. The respected grappler had been around the sport since 1983, won the WCW World tag team title with Rick Steamboat in 1992, and helped establish ECW as a major federation by winning and defending three world heavyweight titles. He called himself "the Franchise." He was a man who got what he wanted. He wanted Torrie, and he got her.

"Little Billy Kidman, there was just something about you that didn't quite please me," Torrie told Kidman at *Nitro*.

Kidman was shocked, insulted, and hurt. He fought back with words.

"What Torrie Wilson doesn't realize is that skanks like her are a dime a dozen," Kidman replied. "She's a gold digger."

That night, Kidman took on Jeff Jarrett in an exciting, fast-paced match. Jarrett scored with a hiptoss over the top rope, then Irish-whipped Kidman into the guardrail. Kidman rallied with a standing dropkick, then rolled up Jarrett for a two-count. Kidman climbed to the top rope and scored with a flying bodypress, but Jarrett reversed the pin and nearly scored a pin of his own. When Kidman threw Jarrett over the top rope, Torrie appeared on the scene with Shane Douglas.

When Billy Kidman showed the Nitro *audience a videotape of Torrie Wilson as an overweight teenager, he ignited a feud with Torrie's new boyfriend, Shane Douglas.*

Kidman desperately needed to maintain his focus. He wanted to beat the recently de-throned WCW World heavyweight champion. Douglas hit Kidman from behind, and Jarrett nearly got the three-count. Kidman rebounded from a powerbomb, but Douglas nailed Kidman from behind. Jarrett scored the pin, and Kidman was furious.

The Kidman vs. Douglas feud turned mean and violent. The wrestlers displayed their immaturity by trading barbs about the woman they supposedly loved.

When Douglas was joined by Torrie for a U.S. title tournament match against Kidman at the July 18, 2000, *Nitro*, Torrie ridiculed Kidman and said she had been using him all along. Kidman stormed the ring. Douglas distracted the referee while Torrie choked Kidman. The battle between Douglas and Kidman spilled outside the ring. Torrie tripped Kidman, and Douglas covered him for a near-fall. Finally, Douglas scored the pin.

Even though he had lost to Douglas, Kidman refused to quiet down. He claimed to have an incriminating tape of himself with Torrie. Suddenly, during a match between Douglas and Mike Awesome, the tape aired on the arena's oversized television screens. A distracted Douglas couldn't believe what he was watching, and Torrie was outraged. Awesome grabbed a metal weight from Torrie and smashed Douglas before scoring the pin. Douglas vowed revenge.

He got his chance the following week in a highly unusual pole match. Kidman and Douglas battled as if they hated each other more than anything else in the world. Torrie climbed onto the ring apron and distracted the referee as Kidman climbed the pole. Douglas attacked Kidman and broke a bottle over his head. The referee turned around, saw Douglas holding the broken bottle, and awarded him the match.

The truth was, though, that Kidman was much madder at Torrie for leaving him than he was at Douglas for stealing her. Torrie's deception hurt far worse than Douglas taking advantage of the opportunity to be with a beautiful woman. After all, hadn't Kidman done the same thing when he had the chance? He had stolen Torrie from David Flair. Kidman realized that by insulting Torrie, he could hurt Douglas and his former valet at the same time.

So that's what he did at *Nitro* on August 7, 2000. The evening started innocently enough, with Kidman taking a seat at the broadcasters' table. He apologized for his personal attacks against Torrie and admitted that he had loved her. Then he declared the evening to be Torrie Appreciation Night. Any fan who had paid attention to Kidman over the last several months knew that Kidman's celebration of Torrie would be anything but a lovefest.

Later in the broadcast, Kidman walked out holding roses, a bottle of champagne, a crown, and a box of candy. He praised and complimented Torrie. *Just maybe,* many fans undoubtedly thought, *Kidman's making a last-ditch effort at winning her back.*

Torrie, standing backstage, watched the proceedings on a video monitor. She seemed genuinely touched by Kidman's gesture and walked out to the ring. Kidman called for a video to be shown on the arena's television monitors. It was hardly a tribute to Torrie. The video showed an overweight, awkward, and much younger Torrie at a birthday party. When the tape ended, copies of Torrie's high school yearbook photos—which were anything but flattering—fluttered down from the arena ceiling.

Enraged, Douglas charged to the ring. Kidman pulled a pair of brass knuckles from the box of chocolates. Torrie went to hit Kidman over the head with the bottle of champagne, but Kidman moved out of the way. Then Reno, the boyfriend of one of the *Nitro* girls, rushed out and attacked Kidman. Douglas took advantage of the opportunity and whipped Kidman with a belt.

At this point, Kidman probably should have taken a step back, examined his situation, and realized that his feud with Douglas was getting him nowhere. Douglas wasn't a champion. The only thing he had that Kidman wanted was Torrie, and he was no longer certain he wanted her, anyway. Douglas vs. Kidman was nothing more than a grudge feud. No titles were at stake, only personal pride.

Both men put their pride on the line again at the *New Blood Rising* pay-per-view on August 13. It was a strap match, in which the two men were strapped together.

"You weren't man enough to keep Torrie," Douglas mocked Kidman, only further infuriating his rival. The action was hot inside and outside the ring. Kidman whipped Douglas into the steel guardrail. When the action returned to the ring, Torrie distracted the referee, and Douglas hit Kidman with a low blow. Kidman rallied with a huracanrana and a powerbomb.

Torrie tried to hit Kidman with her shoe, but struck Douglas instead. Kidman nearly scored the pin. Douglas reversed a cradle attempt for a pin, but Kidman battled back and ultimately scored the win.

The match was over, but the real action had just begun. Torrie stepped into the ring carrying a steel chair. Kidman ducked when she tried to hit him, but Douglas attacked Kidman from behind. Big Vito saved Kidman. Reno joined Douglas. Mayhem broke out in the ring. Clearly, this feud was far from over.

Kidman and Big Vito teamed up against Reno and Douglas at *Nitro* on August 14, 2000. The fans were on Kidman's side and loudly booed Douglas. The four men battled on the arena floor. Big Vito saved Kidman from getting pinned by Reno, then covered Reno for the win. When the match ended and Douglas tried to handcuff Kidman to the top rope, Vito again interfered and handcuffed Douglas.

Different wrestlers started getting involved in the feud. First it was Reno and Big Vito. Then it was Madusa, who battled Torrie to a no contest at *Nitro*. Douglas interfered and had Madusa locked in a submission hold when Kidman saved her from further harm. Promoters wasted no time signing a scaffold match pitting Douglas and Torrie against Kidman and Madusa at Fall Brawl 2000. A scaffold match is one of the most dangerous in wrestling. The wrestlers battle on a scaffold high above the ring. The object is to push your opponents off the scaffold and to the mat far below, then descend the ladder to the bottom. In this case, the match would be even more dangerous: The scaffold would be constructed

Shane Douglas and Torrie Wilson, above, defeated Billy Kidman and Madusa in a terrifying scaffold match at Fall Brawl 2000.

not above the ring, but off to the side, above the arena's stage area. Douglas vowed that both Kidman and Madusa would take the fall at Fall Brawl.

"And if they don't," Douglas said, "I'll refund everyone's money."

But the match nearly didn't happen. Four days before Fall Brawl, on September 13, Kidman and Madusa wrestled Douglas and Torrie. Douglas and Madusa were battling in the ring when Kidman left the apron and chased Torrie through the crowd. He chased her all the way up to the balcony, where Torrie fell over the railing. Torrie held on for dear life, and Kidman threatened to push her off, until Douglas saved her from certain disaster.

The scaffold match took place in Buffalo, New York on September 17. None of the four wrestlers seemed happy about being on top of the scaffold. Douglas and Kidman carefully exchanged punches. The four wrestlers battled on their hands and knees. Madusa tried to push Douglas off the scaffold, but he held on. Douglas got up and tried to piledrive Kidman, but Kidman responded with a back-bodydrop. Madusa tried to climb down the ladder on the side of the scaffold. Douglas attacked Kidman, then chased Madusa down the ladder. Both combatants were on the ladder when Douglas kicked Madusa to the mat placed on the stage far below. She hit the mat with a thud, but somehow escaped injury. Back on top of the scaffold, Torrie delivered a low blow to Kidman. Douglas climbed back to the top, then threw Kidman off the scaffold. Torrie and Douglas climbed down for the win.

That frightening battle should have ended the Shane Douglas vs. Billy Kidman feud. After all, both men had not only risked their own lives, but the lives of their female partners, in an attempt to settle their differences. There seemed to be nothing left to gain. Kidman, despite losing, had proven himself against a man who was 60 pounds bigger and far more experienced. Douglas had fought for his girl-friend and won.

But the feud refused to end. Billy took a brief break from the feud and lost an out-standing match to Jim Duggan. And Douglas took time out to battle Booker T for the WCW World heavyweight title. Kidman interfered, however, and Booker T scored the pin. So much for taking a break from the feud.

Despite his size, Kidman continued to pick fights with heavyweights like fellow New Blood member Scott Steiner.

As if one grudge feud wasn't enough, Kidman inadvertently started another with former New Blood member Scott Steiner. It happened after Kidman accidentally bumped into Midajah, Steiner's valet. Steiner challenged Kidman to a match, and Kidman accepted. Once again, he was dealing with a much bigger man: Steiner is 6' 2", 270 pounds, and is considered one of the strongest men in the world. It seemed logical that Kidman didn't stand a chance, and indeed he didn't. Steiner pummeled Kidman from turnbuckle to turnbuckle and scored an easy victory by submission. Two days later, Steiner scored another submission victory over Kidman.

Many people feel that Kidman made a major mistake by leaving the cruiserweight division and going after the big boys. Why, after all, was Kidman battling men far larger than himself in grudge matches when he could have been dominating "Above Average" Mike Sanders, "Primetime" Elix Skipper, Lance Storm, and others in the cruiserweight title race? After all, Billy Kidman is anything but "above average." He's *far* above average. But Kidman had an answer for the critics.

"Some people who are smaller have a problem," Kidman said in an Internet interview. "They try to wrestle like they are a lot bigger. When you know your size, you are able to put a match together to complement both guys. I certainly am not going to bodyslam Kevin Nash, but there are other ways I can take him off his feet that are believable and make for an entertaining match. Basically, you just have to know your size and how to put a match together. I do know my size, and I don't think I've even begun to have my best matches yet."

Bigger men such as Douglas, Steiner, Hogan, Sting, and Page all know that Kidman never backs down from a challenge. He never takes the easy way out. Billy Kidman isn't content with being the best cruiserweight in the world. He wants to be the best wrestler in the world.

His boast may very well be true. As remarkable as his career has been up to this point, the best may yet lie ahead.

Chronology

1974 Born Pete Gruner in Allentown, Pennsylvania, on May 11

1992 Enters Afa's Wild Samoan Wrestling Training Center

1994 Makes his debut at a small show in Pennsylvania and loses to "Disco" Joey Travolla

1996 Signs his first contract with WCW and takes on the name Billy Kidman

1997 Joins Raven's Flock in October and changes his look from clean-cut to grunge

1998 Makes his pay-per-view debut by wrestling Juventud Guerrera at WCW's Bash at the Beach; Perry Saturn pins Raven to free The Flock. Kidman gets rid of the grunge look; beats Juventud Guerrera for his first WCW cruiserweight title; loses the cruiserweight title to Juventud Guerrera; regains the cruiserweight title from Guerrera

1999 Kidman and Misterio beat Chris Benoit and Dean Malenko for the WCW World tag team title; Kidman and Misterio lose the WCW World tag team title to Perry Saturn and Raven; Kidman and Konnan win the WCW World tag team title from Harlem Heat; Kidman and Konnan lose the WCW World tag team title to Creative Control.

2000 At Nitro, Kidman calls out former world champion Hulk Hogan and pins him in an impromptu match; the New Blood is formed; the Filthy Animals reunite to launch a feud with WCW's Millionaire's Club; Kidman and Madusa lose to Shane Douglas and Torrie in a Fall Brawl scaffold match.

Further Reading

"Billy Kidman." *The Wrestling Analyst* (July 1999): 10–13.

Burkett, Harry. "Talk About Pressure! If Kidman Loses, Torrie Walks!"
    Inside Wrestling (June 2000): 30-33.

Kidman, Billy ("Hotseat" interview). "Hogan's the One Who Belongs
    at a Flea Market." *Inside Wrestling* (September 2000): 42–45.

Rosenbaum, Dave. "Did You Ever Have To Make Up Your Mind? Kidman
    and Misterio Can't Be Friends … And Enemies." *Pro Wrestling Illustrated*
    (September 1999): 40–44.

Rosenbaum, Dave. "Introducing: Kid Flash." *The Wrestler* (June 1996): 18–19.

Tow, Tim. "Size Doesn't Matter: WCW'S Billy Kidman Is No Longer Just a Kid
    in the Wrestling Business." *WOW Magazine* (September 2000): 60–62.

Index

Photo Credits

The Acci'Dent: pp. 2, 6, 30, 34, 37, 60; Jeff Eisenberg Sports Photography: pp. 12, 16, 48;
Howard Kernats Photography: pp. 9, 15, 18, 23, 25, 26, 29, 40, 42, 44, 50, 56, 58.

JACQUELINE MUDGE is a frequent contributor to sports and entertainment magazines in the United States. Born in Idaho, she became a wrestling fan at age 11 when her father took her to matches. Although she has a degree in journalism, she left the writing arena for several years in the late 1980s to pursue a career in advertising sales. She returned to the profession—and the sport she loves—in 1995. Her previously published volumes on the mat sport include *Randy Savage: The Story of the Wrestler They Call "Macho Man"* and *Bret Hart: The Story of the Wrestler They Call "The Hitman."*